Defying Gravity!
ROCK CLIMBING

D0167232

Christine Dugan, M.A.Ed.

Consultants

Timothy Rasinski, Ph.D.
Kent State University

Lori Oczkus
Literacy Consultant

Peter Torcicollo
President of USA Climbin

Based on writing from
TIME For Kids. *TIME For Kids* and the *TIME For Kids* logo are registered trademarks of TIME Inc. Used under license.

Publishing Credits

Dona Herweck Rice, *Editor-in-Chief*
Lee Aucoin, *Creative Director*
Jamey Acosta, *Senior Editor*
Heidi Fiedler, *Editor*
Lexa Hoang, *Designer*
Stephanie Reid, *Photo Editor*
Emily Engle, *Contributing Author*
Rachelle Cracchiolo, *M.S.Ed., Publisher*

Image Credits: p.19 Alamy; p.48 Christine Dugan; pp.38–39 EPA/Newscom; pp.6 (bottom), 30–31, 32 (top & bottom) Getty Images; pp.16–17 (illustrations), pp.20, 26–27 (illustrations) Timothy J. Bradley; pp.9 (bottom right), 10 (bottom), 10–11, 16, 30–32 (upper middle), p.36 (top right) iStockphoto; p.8 (bottom) National Geographic Stock; All other images fromShutterstock.

Teacher Created Materials
5301 Oceanus Drive
Huntington Beach, CA 92649-1030
http://www.tcmpub.com
ISBN 978-1-4333-4830-3
© 2013 Teacher Created Materials, Inc.

Table of Contents

The Climb

A team of climbers stretches. They compare injuries and stories. The red sun is starting to rise. A bird flies by just below. The climb was amazing—the view is unforgettable.

Rock climbing is a sport that requires physical strength, intense focus, and true courage. And it is a sport that people of all ages can try. Rock climbers love facing new challenges. With every climb, they seek new thrills and new views. But the danger of a fall is always possible. The risks are great, but the rewards are awesome. It's time to go **vertical**!

THINK LINK

Think you're ready to try rock climbing? Here are some things you'll need to know about:
- climbing techniques and safety skills
- what gear to grab
- math (even the strongest climbers won't get far without math!)

What to Wear

Rock climbing is fun, but it is also serious business. A climber never just leaves home in the morning dressed in shorts and sneakers and heads to the mountain to climb for the day. This kind of outing takes a lot of planning.

Rock climbing requires special gear. These items help climbers stay safe and comfortable on the climb. What they wear is very important. They want to wear gear that fits correctly and allows their bodies to move while climbing.

Gear Up!

A rock climber purchases gear at an outdoor supply store. Look at the costs to see what items are most expensive. Why do you think that is? How much does the gear shown cost all together?

socks
$4.65

shoes
$75.95

jacket
$59.99

Smart clothing choices also depend on the weather. Clothes may need to be lightweight or waterproof. Wearing layers is always a good choice.

Special climbing shoes help a climber's feet stay steady on the rocks. The shoes should be high enough on the sides to protect the ankles.

Keep Your Head in the Game

A helmet is a very important piece of gear. A climber must wear it in order to stay safe. Just as a bike helmet makes it safer to ride a bike, a climbing helmet protects a climber's head.

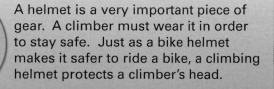

gloves
$12.99

helmet
$29.99

= **Total?**

Rope Up!

Climbers carry special equipment to **scale** a mountain of any height. The gear allows climbers to move up a vertical wall of rock. Yet it does something even more essential than that. It keeps climbers from falling!

The most useful piece of climbing equipment is a **harness**. A harness is made of a set of straps, belt loops, and buckles. The straps secure a climber to a piece of rope. The harness allows a climber to climb up and down while safely tied to a partner. Rock climbing ropes come in a variety of sizes, shapes, and weights. Experienced climbers use different ropes for different climbs.

Climbers also carry chalk. But they aren't writing or drawing with it. Chalk helps a climber grip the rock. It dries sweaty hands. The chalk is kept in a chalk bag. This is usually attached to the climber's belt.

Chalk helps sweaty hands grip rocks.

belt

harness

helmet

chalk bag

rope

Safety Check

Inspecting gear before each climb is very important. Climbers should look for any signs of wear and tear. Climbing equipment needs to be replaced **periodically** (peer-ee-OD-ik-lee) to keep it in good working condition. If equipment fails, the consequences could be deadly.

Making the Grade

Planning ahead before a climb makes for a safer experience. Knowing about proper clothing and gear is key. So is deciding how long to climb and how difficult the trail should be.

One thing to consider is the distance of a climb. Climbers must know ahead of time how far they are climbing. This impacts the kinds of items a climber needs to carry. Weather also **influences** what to pack.

It is important to choose a route with the right amount of challenge. Many climbers look at how steep the climb will be. Climbers can also study what skills will be needed for the climb. They may need to practice new skills before the next big climb.

65°
angle

51°
angle

Awesome Angles

17°
angle

**Rock walls
and mountains
can have a gradual
slope to them. These are easier
climbs and perfect for taking in
the view. The most extreme climbs
are totally vertical. What can you handle?**

72°
angle

Taking It to the Next Level

Rock climbing routes are **graded** so climbers can predict how difficult the climb will be. In the United States, climbs range from class 1.0 to class 5.5. The chart below details the challenging 5.1–5.5 range. If you can handle a 5.3 climb in the U.S., what level can you handle in Australia? What about in Germany?

United States	France	Australia	South Africa	Germany
5.1	2	7	8	III-
5.2	2+	8	9	III
5.3	3	9–10	10	III+
5.4	3+	11	12	IV-
5.5	4	12	13	IV

Class 1
Trail Walking

includes flat rocky paths with trails

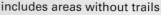

Class 2
Off-Trail Hiking

includes areas without trails

**Class 5
Technical Climbing**

requires advanced
skills; includes some
overnight climbs

**Class 3
Scrambling**

hands are used to
climb and hike

**Class 4
Easy Climbing**

climbing equipment can be
required; covers steeper areas

The Challenge

Before a climb, climbers must train physically. Rock climbing is a sport for people of all ages. The people who enjoy it the most are in good physical health. A climber's body needs to be ready for a vigorous workout.

Training is important in all sports. Rock climbers can train in different ways. They may train indoors to prepare for a mountain climb. Rock-climbing gyms are a great place for climbers to visit before a big climb. Doing a workout for the hands and fingers may sound strange. Yet it actually helps strengthen them before grabbing hold of rocks. Strength exercises for leg and arm muscles are important, too.

Training Schedule

Look at this sample training schedule below. This climber is getting ready for a challenging climb in three weeks. How many hours is she training each week? How many total hours will she train?

Week One					
Monday Climbing gym 5:00–7:00	**Tuesday** Rest	**Wednesday** Climbing gym 5:00–6:00	**Thursday** Regular gym 4:00–5:00	**Friday** Regular gym 5:00–6:00	**Saturday** Climb Mt. Wilson 8:00–11:00
Week Two					
Monday Climbing gym 5:00–7:00	**Tuesday** Rest	**Wednesday** Climbing gym 5:00–7:00	**Thursday** Regular gym 5:00–6:30	**Friday** Regular gym 4:00–5:30	**Saturday** Climb Mt. Peakon 7:00–10:30
Week Three					
Monday Climbing gym 4:00–7:00	**Tuesday** Rest	**Wednesday** Climbing gym 4:30–7:30	**Thursday** Regular gym 4:00–6:30	**Friday** Regular gym 6:00–8:30	**Saturday** Climb Mt. Olympionus 6:00–10:30

Summit!

Rock On

Get a Grip!

Rock climbers use different words to describe how they can grip a rock. These **handholds** can be called **gaston**, **pinch**, **sloper**, **crimp**, **undercling**, or **jug** holds.

gaston

The planning is done. The mountain is waiting. It's time for a climb!

Serious rock climbers practice different climbing techniques. For example, climbers might choose between **edging** or **flagging** foot techniques. Edging uses the inside of the foot to stand, while flagging uses one foot dangled behind the other to improve balance.

Using different parts of the feet can be helpful, too. A **heel hook** means the climber is using the heel to pull up. A **toe hook** means hooking the toe onto the rock.

Climbers also learn how to use their hands and feet at the same time. Sometimes, they find it is even better to switch between them. All these choices help a climber move more easily up the rock.

pinch

sloper

crimp

undercling

jug

Navigating the Distance

Rock climbers are adventurous. They love being outdoors. They crave the feeling that comes when they complete a great climb. There's no match for the amazing view at the top of a cliff. A trip can be a short few hours of physical activity. It can also be a several-day **excursion**. Distance should be considered before the climb.

Climbers think about where they want to go and how far they want to climb. They take into account what level of difficulty they are ready to tackle. For longer trips, they need to bring along food and sleeping gear.

Trail maps can be helpful in deciding on the distance of a climbing trip. Climbers can study the maps to decide where to make stops. These stops give climbers a break and make the trip easier.

Global positioning system (GPS) devices can help climbers find the location of a climb they want to take.

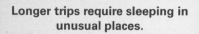

Longer trips require sleeping in unusual places.

DIG DEEPER!

On the Map

This trail guide shows the distance a climber might travel during a climbing trip. Look at the map and the scale. Determine how far the climber will travel during the trip using the different routes listed below.

forest

campground

vista point

1 = beginner walk

2 = lake view trail

3 = forest's edge

4 = extreme heights

5 = challenging pass

NORTH

5

4

1 inch = 1 mile

The Ultimate Climb

The great climber George Mallory was asked why he wanted to climb Mt. Everest. His answer: "Because it is there."

Good Grub

Rock climbing is hard work for the body! It requires people to carefully plan how much food and water they will need. Climbers must **replenish** the energy that they use. They also must choose foods that help them stay focused and healthy. Trail mix is an easy snack to carry.

Before the climb, climbers eat and drink in order to prevent **dehydration** (dee-hayh-DREY-shuhn) and fatigue (fuh-TEEG). The closer they get to the climb, the less they may want to eat. Climbing requires a healthy diet. **Carbohydrates** (kahr-boh-HAYH-dreytz) made from whole grains are a good choice. So are fruits and vegetables. Protein from nuts or lean meats will also help climbers get the energy they need.

Smart Snacks

Climbers carry their own snacks to refuel while they are out on the mountain. Crackers, pretzels, trail mix, string cheese, and dried fruit are just some of the healthy foods that make good snacks.

Burning Calories

A 90-pound child who rock climbs burns approximately 450 calories in an hour. An ounce of almonds has around 170 calories and a banana has about 80 calories. If the child eats an ounce of almonds and a banana, how many calories does the child eat? How many more calories does the child burn than what he or she eats?

Under the Stars

Some climbers enjoy taking longer trips, so they need to plan where they will sleep. A trail may allow climbers to sleep in a tent on flat land. They may get to the top of a peak and then rest and sleep before going on. Sometimes, climbers will decide to **ascend** a long peak that takes several days to climb. Where do they sleep on these types of trips? On the side of the mountain, of course! A **portaledge** is a tent that can be attached to the side of a rock.

Packing Light

Climbers on overnight trips must carry whatever they need. The weight of their packs is important. If a climber takes a 4-day trip, how many meals does the climber need to bring? If a day's worth of food weighs 1.2 pounds, how much will 4 days of food weigh?

Can you find the words that make up *portaledge*? It's the perfect way to describe a portable ledge!

Extreme Exposure

Waterproof, layered clothing prevents climbers from getting too cold or wet. Keeping hands and fingers warm is especially important. Exposure to cold temperatures can result in **hypothermia** (hahy-puh-THUR-mee-uh) or frostbite.

DIG DEEPER!

Learn the Lingo

Rock climbers have a language all their own. Do you want to read more about rock climbing or share stories with a rock climber? You will have to learn the lingo! Knowing some of these terms will help you understand the world of rock climbing and the language used in it.

belaying (bih-LEY-ing)—securing a rock climber at one end of the rope

carabiner (kar-uh-BEE-ner)—a D-shaped metal ring that connects a rope to an anchor in a rock or to another rope

crux—the most difficult move during a climb

dirt me—a term climbers use to tell the belayer they want to be lowered to the ground

fingerboard—a training device that strengthens a climber's grip and arm strength

flake—a piece of rock that is chipped off a rock face but is still connected; it is dangerous for a climber if he or she tries to grip a flake, as it could break off the rock face

gumby—an amateur (AM-uh-choor) rock climber

jamming—a technique in which climbers wedge their hands or feet inside a gap in a rock in order to get a grip

monkey toe—a technique where climbers use their toes to latch on to the surface of a rock in order to get a grip and continue climbing

piton (PEE-ton)—a metal spike with an eye that is jammed into the rock, providing anchors to which climbers attach their ropes

rappelling (ra-PEL-ing)—a technique used to safely move to the bottom of a rock

top out—to reach the top of a climbing wall; to sit at the top of a climbing wall

Fear Factor

Rock climbing is a dangerous sport. It is crucial to think about safety at all times.

Why do climbers fall? Most falls happen because of climber error. Sometimes, climbers fall because their gear breaks or fails in some way. Checking gear is important for safety reasons. Climbers watch for signs of wear and tear. They replace ropes and other materials when they are getting worn.

Tackling a difficult climb can also lead to injury. Climbers should only climb where they can do so safely.

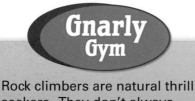

Gnarly Gym

Rock climbers are natural thrill seekers. They don't always want to be safe and take things easy. Yet trying out new tricks or daring moves is best saved for an indoor climbing gym with mats that protect against falls.

Pro Performance

One way to prevent rock climbing accidents is to train with professionals. Learning about the sport from people who know a lot about safety is a great way to avoid hazardous situations.

Rescuers carefully bring an injured climber down a mountain.

Free Fall

The most common injuries after a fall are **sprains**, cuts, and breaks. These injuries usually happen to feet, legs, or backs. Being in the wild with an injury is dangerous. For safety reasons, climbers should never climb alone. A climbing partner can give first aid or go get help. Cell phones may not work. Some climbers like to have a **locator beacon** or a GPS of some kind.

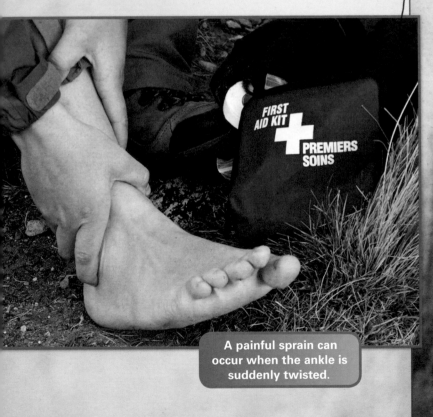

A painful sprain can occur when the ankle is suddenly twisted.

A Rock and a Hard Place

A popular film, *127 Hours*, tells the story of Aron Ralston. Ralston was climbing alone in a canyon in Utah when an 800-pound boulder shifted and pinned his hand against the wall. After being trapped for six days, he finally freed himself by cutting off his own arm. Despite this injury, he still enjoys rock climbing.

Maximum Impact

The chart below shows some injuries that could happen on a climb. It also tells what kind of first aid can make a difference in a tough situation. It's important to be able to help a fellow climber after a fall. Knowing about first aid and CPR is one way to assist. This can keep a climber safe until help is on the way.

If

If a climber sprains a wrist or ankle...

If a climber has a bad cut...

If a climber has a broken bone...

If a climber falls and cannot move...

Then

...keep the wrist or ankle still. Put ice on the injury, if possible. Wrap the injury in a spare T-shirt or sock.

...put direct pressure on the cut. Use a bandage or a clean piece of clothing. If the cut stops bleeding, clean with an alcohol wipe from a first aid kit.

...keep the body part with the broken bone still. If possible, make a **splint**. Use a strong, straight stick and bandages or a clean piece of clothing. Straighten the body part against the stick. Wrap the bandage or clothing around and tie it together.

...keep the person still, especially the head and neck. Do not try to move the fall victim.

Going
Vertical

Rock climbers love their sport. They travel all around the world to experience new climbs. Everyone has a favorite place to climb.

The southwestern United States is known for its gorgeous rocks and canyons. Italy and Greece offer beautiful views for climbers. Australia and New Zealand are also popular places to climb.

Traveling for rock climbing is exciting. Yet many climbers are just as happy with a big rock and a pretty view. They can find that anywhere!

Conquer the Climb

The sport of rock climbing may include several different types of climbing. Indoor climbing, traditional climbing, bouldering (BOHL-der-ing), sport climbing, and ice climbing are all ways that rock climbers choose to climb up something!

Bouldering

These climbs take place at low levels on large rocks without any ropes. A mat called a *crash pad* is placed below the rocks. This protects the climber in case of a fall.

Indoor Climbing

These climbs are made on artificial (ahr-tuh-FISH-uhl) rock faces. It gives the feeling of climbing outdoors, but in a safe indoor gym.

Traditional Climbing

A climber places anchors in the rock to climb. As the climber descends the rock, he or she removes the anchors that were placed.

Sport Climbing

Climbers use anchors or bolts that are already placed in the rock. They clip onto them with metal hangers. Climbers don't need to place the anchors themselves, so they can focus on making the difficult climbing moves.

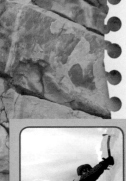

Ice Climbing

Climbers scale a frozen surface, such as a frozen waterfall or a glacier. They use picks to grab hold of the icy surface as they climb.

STOP! THINK...

- Which type of climbing looks most exciting to you?
- Which type of climbing do you think is easiest for beginners?
- Where might you go to try these different types of climbs?

The Greatest Climber in the World

People think that Reinhold (RAHYN-hohld) Messner is the greatest mountain climber of all time. He has done things during his climbing career that others only dream of. One of his most famous feats is climbing Mount Everest, the tallest mountain in the world, without using extra oxygen.

Most climbers need the extra oxygen. This is because the air at the top of the mountain has very little oxygen. The low oxygen and physical exertion makes it a very tough climb. Most people cannot survive this. But Reinhold Messner did!

"Who knows what freedom is? No one.
I often think that we mountaineers get
nearest to it, this paradise on Earth."

—Reinhold Messner, professional rock climber

Dare to Succeed

Rock climbers push their bodies to the limit to do what they love. They see places many people will never see. They know sweat and pain. They also know how to stay focused, fight fear, and train their bodies to do whatever it takes to reach the top. Smart climbers are safe and careful. But all climbers deserve our respect for their hard work. And there's always a new adventure to try!

"It's good to have an end to journey toward; but it is the journey that matters in the end."

—Ursula K. Le Guin, author

Glossary

ascend—climb up something

carbohydrates—a source of energy for the body found in foods such as bread and fruits

crimp—a grip used to hold a small ledge

dehydration—a dangerous lack of water in the body

edging—a climbing technique that uses the inside of the foot to stand

excursion—a journey made for pleasure

flagging—a climbing technique that uses one foot dangled behind the other to improve balance

gaston—a handhold that must be gripped with the palm facing away, thumb down, and elbow out; similar to opening a sliding glass door

Global Positioning System (GPS)—a satellite-based navigation system that provides locations

graded—given a value to indicate difficulty

harness—a set of straps used to fasten a person to something

heel hook—a foot technique in which climbers use their heel to pull up

handholds—places to grip the rock

hypothermia—a dramatic lowering of one's body temperature

influences—acts on something in a way that produces an effect

jug—a large handhold that is easy to grab

locator beacon—a device used to send a distress signal from remote places

periodically—at regular times

pinch—a small or large handhold that is gripped by pinching it with the hand

portaledge—a portable tent that can be attached to the side of a rock during a long climb to provide a place for a climber to rest or sleep

replenish—to make complete again by supplying what is lacking

scale—to climb up something

sloper—a sloping handhold gripped like a basketball

splint—a strip of rigid material used to keep an arm or leg in a fixed position

sprains—painful injuries to the ligaments of a joint

toe hook— a foot technique in which climbers hook their toe onto the rock

undercling—a handhold of rock gripped with the palm facing upwards

vertical—at a right angle to the horizon; upright

Index

Bibliography

Greve, Tom. *Rock Climbing.* **Rourke Publishing, 2009.**
This book will give you key information on the sport of rock climbing. Photographs throughout the book help explain the information.

Long, Denise. *Survivor Kid: A Practical Guide to Wilderness Survival.* **Chicago Review Press, 2011.**
This book explains a variety of survival skills and techniques to kids, including how to build a shelter, important navigation skills, and how to stay safe if you encounter wild animals.

Roberts, Jeremy. *Rock and Ice Climbing!* **The Rosen Publishing Group, Inc., 2000.**
Learn about rock climbing and ice climbing, including safety tips, equipment needed, the history of the sport, and famous climbers.

Salkeld, Audrey. *Climbing Everest: Tales of Triumph and Tragedy on the World's Highest Mountain.* **National Geographic Children's Books, 2003.**
Learn about the history of climbers who have tackled Mount Everest, one of the world's highest and most difficult climbs. Each chapter tells the detailed story of one climber or climbing team as they experience successes or failures during their journey.

Seeberg, Tim. *Rock Climbing: Kids' Guides to the Outdoors.* **The Child's World, 2004.**
This book is a beginner's look at the world of rock climbing. Important information on safety and rock climbing equipment is included.

More to Explore

Rock Climbing for Life
www.rock-climbing-for-life.com

See videos of rock climbers, view photos of beautiful landscapes, and read articles from expert rock climbers at this website.

Rock Climbing
www.rockclimbing.com

This website is a place where you can connect with rock climbers. Photos, videos, and discussions are all posted here.

Yahoo! Kids
http://kids.yahoo.com/directory/sports-and-recreation/outdoors/mountain-climbing

This website lists many interesting articles and websites that will tell you more about rock climbing, climbs in different parts of the world, famous climbers, and gear.

Encyclopedia Britannica for Kids
http://kids.britannica.com/

Encyclopedia Britannica online provides you with a searchable database of information on any content that you are studying in class or that you would like to know more about. These entries are written for ages 8–11 or 11 and up.

Teacher Tube
http://teachertube.com

Teachertube.com is a safe website for your teachers to look up videos to use in your classrooms studying. You can find great videos of rock-climbing events here.

About the Author

Christine Dugan earned her B.A. from the University of California, San Diego. She taught elementary school for several years before deciding to take on a different challenge in the field of education. She has worked as a product developer, writer, editor, and sales assistant for various educational publishing companies. In recent years, Christine earned her master's degree in education and is currently working as a freelance author and editor. She lives with her husband and two daughters in the Pacific Northwest, where she loves to explore the view.